CONTENTS

ACKNOWLEDGEMENTS

We would like to thank Jean Taylor, Joyce Miller and Evelyn Whitfield for their invaluable help in putting this book together.

Miles Tubb and John McCaughie

BRITAIN IN OLD PHOTOGRAPHS

EDINBURGH

MILES TUBB & JOHN McCAUGHIE

The
History
Press

A snapshot of Edinburgh in the early 1950s. This picture gives a wonderful overview of Princes Street, from the top of the Scott Monument looking east towards Calton Hill. To the right is the old Waverley Market, where fruit and vegetables used to be sold, with the North British Hotel, now the Balmoral Hotel, behind it. The old market was replaced by a modern shopping centre in the 1980s. Opposite Waverley Market, on the corner of South St Andrew Street, is R.W. Forsyth's, the prestigious Edinburgh clothing store. The awnings are out over the shops and the trams are still running along Princes Street. (Photograph donated by Margaret Brown)

First published 2011

The History Press
The Mill, Brimscombe Port
Stroud, Gloucestershire, GL5 2QG
www.thehistorypress.co.uk

© Miles Tubb & John McCaughie 2011

British Library Cataloguing in Publication Data.
A catalogue record for this book is available from the British Library.

ISBN 978 0 7524 5918 9

Typesetting and origination by The History Press
Printed in Great Britain
Manufacturing managed by Jellyfish Print Solutions

INTRODUCTION

At the time of writing there has been a major shift in photography – the digital age is upon us. Nearly all of the major manufacturers have stopped making film cameras to concentrate on digital products. Film itself is harder to come by in shops, and photographers now speak of megapixels, memory cards, and start-up times. Instead of a photograph being 'grainy' or 'fuzzy, it has 'noise'.

The majority of the images in this booklet are the result of a previous photographic revolution, one that popularised the personal use of the medium by the masses for the first time. It began in the United States with a fledgling company called Kodak. Their idea was simple and was almost the forerunner to disposable cameras: they would sell you a reasonably-priced camera, pre-loaded with film. Once you had taken your photographs, you returned the camera to Kodak, who would process and print your images. The results were returned, along with the camera, once again loaded with film.

It didn't take too long before the process was made simpler by the development of a small, box-like camera called a 'Brownie'. You now bought the film from the chemist and loaded it yourself. The same chemist or photographic dealer would then process the film: the 'snap' was born.

Of course, not everyone was able to afford even this, but the majority of families would have managed to gather a few snaps for the family album. The Living Memory Association archive is largely composed of these snaps, donated by ordinary people. Why? What possible interest could they have outside of a family or personal collection, these photographs of holidays, school classes, weddings, family gatherings, and, of course, children? Unfamiliar faces stare out at us in fashions that have long since passed; their only worth must surely be as oddities.

There is a saying that, 'the local is the only universal', and this has been a good starting point for the archive. Snaps celebrate the ordinary; they show events to which we can all relate. A 1930s' photograph of a Sunday school picnic in Edinburgh would probably trigger memories for someone of a similar age from Exeter. They also have the power to contrast: a 1920s' class photo, where pupils are in bare feet, will come as a shock to the Nike trainer-clad children of today.

My colleague John McCaughie has coined the phrase, 'ordinary lives lived through extraordinary times', to describe those who lived through the Second World War. However, I think it also perfectly describes the majority of the people with whom we work, who have not only lived through wars but also through huge social, economic and technological changes. Throughout an often turbulent century people went to school, started work, went to the cinema, danced, courted, married; just went about the business of living. I hope our archive, and this book, reflect that. I hope it really does celebrate the ordinary.

The Living Memory Association (LMA) is an unique organisation in Scotland which exists to promote oral and community history by various means, including reminiscence groups and training, publications, exhibitions, and our photographic archive. The archive provides an enchanting glimpse into the social history of Edinburgh and beyond. The photographs described in this book were kindly donated to the LMA by people we've interviewed on a one-to-one basis and worked with in reminiscence groups.

The Living Memory Association is grateful to the Big Lottery for funding much of this work.

ONE

ART OF THE SNAP

A photograph from a photographer's studio in Edinburgh in the 1900s; this is one of the more elaborate sets showing one of Scotland's most famous landmarks, the Forth Rail Bridge. Sets and props were important in the early days of photography, as they helped to frame the subject and allow them to keep steady for the long exposure times. (Postcard)

This is a creased studio portrait from the 1920s. The fashion is very much of the time; the men's 'bunnets' are particularly evocative of the inter-war years. The man holding the duckling on a stick is Magnus Houston. It could have been the photographer's prop for 'Watch the birdie'; or could it be the mascot of a bird-watching team? (Photograph donated by Barbara Jeffrey)

Cathy Lyle pictured with her husband at Warriston allotments, in Edinburgh, in the 1930s. The substantial-looking shed in the picture was built by Cathy's husband. He obviously put a lot of hard work into it and it's been decorated like a wee cottage, with a picket fence running round. Maybe this was their dream cottage in miniature. The allotments are thought to have their origins in the 'common land' allocated to the poor in the Middle Ages. The peak of their popularity was during the Second World War, when food production was of national importance. (Photograph donated by Cathy Lyle)

An Edinburgh studio photograph dated 1919. An otherwise ordinary photograph made unusual by the writing on the photo: 'I leave all to her' and the man's signature, Laurence Vymer. This is Laurence's attempt to manipulate the photograph into some kind of visual will! Sadly it was not legally binding and the wording is certainly offhand, 'I leave all to her' rather than 'I leave all to my lovely wife'. (Photograph donated by Eric and June Grainger)

This is Willie B. Jarvie, photographed in 1945, standing outside Willie Liston's barber shop in Main Street, Newhaven. Willie Liston was well known for popping next door to the pub, for a swift one, half-way through shaving a customer with a cut-throat razor. Sounds like it would be a tense time for the customer in the chair, and probably a fairly relaxed time for Willie. (Photograph donated by George Hackland)

This is a photograph of Owen Charles Wilton, taken in the Lawnmarket, Edinburgh, in 1920. The photographer's use of light and shadow make this portrait stand out: a 'box brownie' masterpiece. (Photograph donated by Maisie Mitchell)

A wonderfully composed interior shot in the kitchen of 42 Dumbiedykes Road, Edinburgh. Notice the black lead grate in the background. The photograph was taken with a 'box brownie', resting on the table top. The woman dominates the photo; the teacup and the biscuit poised in her hand add to the overall effect. (Photograph donated by Jean Bell)

A May Day service, on top of Arthur's Seat, on 1 May 1947 or 1948. The ceremony, at dawn, involved people washing their hands and face in the morning dew, in the hope that this would make them more beautiful! The man on the right with his hands stretched out is Revd Selby-Wright, from the Canongate. He was rather jokingly referred to as 'seldom-right'. (Photograph donated by Joan Dougan)

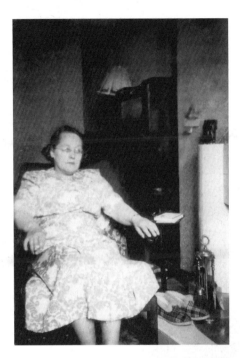

Companion pieces: 'Her indoors' and 'Him indoors' at Piershill Place, Edinburgh. These two photographs show the minutiae of domestic life in the early 1950s. It may even be viewed as dated by the style standards of the time. The open fire is very 1930s and in the background, on a high shelf, is a Bakelite radio. You can also just make out a bed-recess in the background of the photo, which allowed the living room to double up as a bedroom. This was a common feature in small, often overcrowded, tenement flats. And you can see her 'baffies' warming by the fire. There's also a 'companion set' by the fire: brush, shovel and tongs. (Photograph donated by Catriona Anderson)

The cast of a local drama group in the 1940s. The stage make-up gives some of them a rather scary appearance. The character on the far right certainly has the look of Lon Chancey about him. The photograph's donor has a brother in the cast, David, who is playing the minister; her cousin is the maid. (Photograph donated by Janet Dalgleish)

An interior shot of a living room from the 1960s. The coal fire has been blocked up and replaced with a coal-effect electric fire. It's certainly cleaner and easier to use, but it looks bland and lacks the warmth of an open hearth. The cat doesn't seem bothered as long as it's warm. There's also a bonsai Christmas tree by the side of the fire. (Photograph donated by Catriona Anderson)

A Victorian stereographic view of Edinburgh, taken from Calton Hill looking west along Princes Street. Stereo views were very popular with the Victorians. Two identical images were taken of a scene; the resulting postcard-size print was then viewed through a simple stereo viewer. The effect was impressively three dimensional. The large building to the left was Calton Gaol, which was demolished in 1938 and replaced by St Andrew's House. (Photograph donated by Hazel Gray)

Another Victorian stereo view of South Bridge, taken from the area close to the bottom of Chambers Street; in the far distance, is the tower of the Tron Church. There are innumerable stories or scenarios unfolding here: two men are stopping for a chat; a woman, resplendent in Victorian finery, walks away from the camera, her long, full skirt trailing the ground. Walking towards her is a man, weighed down by a large box on his back. Heading towards us, in the middle of the road, are two horse-drawn omnibuses. A slice of life, forever frozen in time. The street is still a busy thorough fare today. (Photograph donated by Hazel Gray)

Alex Kendal on his Royal Enfield in 1938; a machine to be proud of. The bright sunlight picks out three tiers of iron railings; most were probably removed during the Second World War to help with the war effort. The background scene shows an example of some typical Edinburgh housing of the time. (Photograph donated by Peggy Kendal)

Photographer's studio, Edinburgh, in the 1890s; a Victorian studio-portrait of the Letters-Kirk family. The formality of the image belies the colourful occupations of some of the family. Will, second right, was a songwriter. His mother Mary, next to him, entertained in picture houses as a singer and dancer. The woman on the far left, Will's wife, was Kim Ballenby, who was a professional dancer. (Photograph donated by May Tully)

Opposite below: This photograph is a battered and creased image from the first decade of the twentieth century. Joey Robertson, the husband of the donor of this photograph, is perched upon a very ornate motorbike. Oil must have seeped into his veins because he went on to run a garage in Hopetoun Crescent, in Edinburgh, in the future.

TWO

CHILDHOOD

A group of boys from the Royal High School are pictured at Middleton Camp in 1967. This was a popular venue for school outings. It was a residential school camp just outside Gorebridge, Midlothian, and pupils from Edinburgh schools visited it for a variety of indoor and outdoor activities. Boys and girls slept in large dormitories on army-style bunk beds. During the day they attended lectures, went on field trips, played team games, and made friends with pupils from other schools. (Photograph donated by Joan Dougan)

Dr Bell's School in Leith, 1923. Sixth from the left, second row down, is Jeremiah Borthwick, who looks healthy, bright and well fed. However, many of the other pupils don't look as though they were faring so well. This area of Leith contained some very poor housing and poverty was common. There is an almost haunted look in some of the children's faces. The boy at the very front left has had most of his head shaved, undoubtedly as the result of having had ringworm. Dr Bell's building still exists and is now a nursery school and community venue. It is situated in Great Junction Street, Leith. (Photograph donated by Barbara Borthwick)

A group of children beside a wall in woodland, near Edinburgh, in the 1890s. The style of clothes that the children are wearing dates the picture to the late nineteenth century. The photograph was taken by one of the Walker family from Bell's Mill in Edinburgh. It's an informal and unusual pose, refreshingly natural compared with the more usual studio portrait of the time. Bell's Mill was a water-powered mill on the Water of Leith, near the Dean Village. (Photograph donated by Lawrence Walker)

Ella and Diane Kent at Leith Links, in 1960. Leith Links has a long and venerable history. It is mentioned in the earliest documentary reference to golf in 1458. King James II tried to ban golf, along with football, as it was interfering with archery practice. The Links was also the headquarters of Oliver Cromwell's army in 1656. It has always been a well-used community space: not much in the way of golf played, but plenty of football and even cricket! It was also the final destination of the annual Leith Hospital parade, which started in 1907. (Photograph donated by Diane Kent)

Peter Bottomley is swinging from a lamp post at the corner of Dumbiedykes Lane and Dumbiedykes Road, Edinburgh. This photograph was taken in 1954 and he is dangling from a gas lamp. In Edinburgh, the person who lit the gas lamps was called 'Leerie the Lamplighter'. The Lamplighter was made famous in the poem by Robert Louis Stevenson. (Photograph donated by Jean Bell)

My tea is nearly ready and the sun has left the sky;
It's time to take the window to see Leerie going by;
For every night at teatime and before you take your seat,
With lantern and with ladder he comes posting up the street.

From 'The Lamplighter' by R.L.S

Betty Chapman's daughter (left) outside Milton House School, Canongate, Edinburgh, in the 1950s. They're laughing in the photo, in spite of the fact that it looks as if they're locked up behind bars for the night. The one in the middle definitely looks guilty of something. It makes a refreshing change to see the children laughing, as all too often people kept a serious expression on their faces while having their picture taken. The school has been re-named and is now known as the Royal Mile Primary School. The school is perfectly sited to take advantage of the wealth of cultural and historical opportunities presented on the Royal Mile – not to mention the Scottish Parliament, which is just a stone's throw away. (Photograph donated by Betty Chapman)

An interior shot showing Peter and Elizabeth Bottomley in their kitchen at 42 Dumbiedykes Road, Edinburgh, in 1954. Almost in a parody of an old married couple, Peter reads his paper (*The Topper* comic) and Elizabeth avoids conversation by feigning sleep. Notice the Bakelite radio on the sideboard in the background. The radio was old-fashioned even by 1954 standards; you can imagine the declaration of war being broadcast from it in 1939. (Photograph donated by Jean Bell)

A child is playing on a tricycle, *c.* 1950. It is a bit of a relic from the past – a recycled cycle! A very neat youngster sits astride the contraption, woolly jumper, scarf, white socks and shorts, all clean as a whistle.

Millie and Margaret Notman in Tennant Street, Leith in 1956. A back green or, more accurately, a backyard. It's a sunny day and we can see the shadow of the photographer. A simple family snapshot that gives some wee snippets of social history. A battered galvanised dustbin, well used; a bicycle wheel hanging above the women's head. Most intriguing is the bench the woman is sitting on. Obviously a recycled item: what was it? A classroom form? A bench from an omnibus or tram? (Photograph donated by Diane Kent)

This photograph shows (left to right) Bill McLean, Colin Aston and Lawrence Irvine, at the annual Scout camp of the 14th Portobello Scout Troop, in 1958, at Jedburgh in the Borders. The Scouts offered boys the chance of an adventure holiday, under canvas, eating sausages around the camp fire and singing Scout songs. The movement originally began as a scheme outlined in *Scouting for Boys* by Baden-Powell. It was intended to supplement the programmes of youth organisations that were already in existence at the time, like the Boys' Brigade and the Boys' Clubs. (Photograph donated by Bill McLean)

The Girl Guide troop from the Guthrie Memorial Church, Easter Road, Edinburgh. They are pictured at Guide camp in 1934. Girl Guides have been around since 1910 – ever since Baden-Powell, the founder of the Scout movement, was inundated with requests from girls to establish a girls' equivalent. Such was the enthusiasm for Guiding that it soon spread worldwide, and since those early days countless millions have made the Guide Promise. Today there are 10 million girls and women in Guiding worldwide. (Photograph donated by Roberta Cowe)

Four children pictured standing against the wall of Dobson Moles Works in St Clair Road, Edinburgh. From the left we have Maisie and Etta Groat, then Douglas and Mary Scott. It's a photograph from 1925. (Photograph donated by Roberta Cowe)

Right: Sylvia, Robert and Kay are pictured in their overalls, ready to paint a fence. This photograph was taken around 1946 in Granton, Edinburgh. It could have been taken straight out of *The Adventures of Tom Sawyer*, or *Huckleberry Finn*. (Photograph donated by Ella Rattan)

Below: Here are Joan and her brother Stuart, unwrapping presents at Christmas in the mid-1950s. As you can see, cowboy outfits were popular for the boys. A popular present for the girls would have been a doll or a doll's house. Many people remember getting an apple and an orange in their stocking and not much else! Christmas for some families in the '50s would include a trip to Santa's Grotto in Patrick Thomson's or Jenner's department stores. (Photograph donated by Joan Dougan)

Evelyn Sime, in her Girl Guide uniform, 1955. Evelyn says: 'The uniform was a bright blue cotton tunic, worn with a leather belt and buckle. (Later, older Guides were allowed to wear the tunic tucked into a navy skirt). The tie was bright yellow and had to be folded and knotted correctly. The metal badge had to be polished with Brasso and pinned on. The embroidered badge showed I was in the Chaffinch Patrol. The beret was navy. The calendar on the wall was a Guide Association one. And the flying duck was one of a set of three which were fashionable at the time.' (Photograph and memory donated by Evelyn Whitfield)

Betty Anderson's children in the back green of 17 Murdoch Terrace, Edinburgh, in 1948. The children are well turned out, especially the girl with her dress coat on. It may have been their Sunday best. Usually children didn't get out to play on the Sabbath; they would go to church, and then maybe go for a walk or visit relatives. There was a wash-house at 19 Murdoch Terrace and, many years before, it had been the scene of a murder. (Photograph donated by Betty Anderson)

Lorraine and Colin Welsh on holiday at Earlsferry, near Elie, Fife in 1962. Beach huts, like the ones in the photo, are still around and, in some areas, have become something of a collector's item. There's a billowing windbreak in the photograph which could be seen as a necessity on a Scottish beach in the summertime. Notice that the children, playing happily in the sand with their buckets and spades, are wearing warm jumpers – typical apparel for a summer's day in Scotland. (Photograph donated by Lorraine Paton)

Just squeezing into the picture is Ella Kent with her children, Derek, Richard and baby Diane, out for a Sunday afternoon walk in 1961. A recreational walk was very much part of life at one time; a cheap and, of course, healthy pastime. Even courting would involve a lot of walking with each other, possibly with more stops though! The picture has an almost hypnotic quality to it. (Photograph donated by Diane Kent)

Shona Mackintosh and a school friend on the boating pond in St Margaret's Loch in Holyrood Park, Edinburgh, in 1969. Nowadays the loch is home to families of geese and swans, but for many years it was a very popular venue for boating. At one time there was a small hut and wooden landing area at the north-east corner of the loch. (Photograph donated by Betty Mackintosh)

Above: Jean Douglas is the child at the front left of this photograph, taken in 1962 at Jewel Cottages. The cottages were on the east side of Niddrie Road, just north of Bingham Railway Bridge. The small wooden door in the wall was a coal bunker. Jean Douglas' dad was a miner and so the family got free coal. There are only two cars in sight; these were the days when it was safe to play in the street. The blur at the bottom of the photograph is a fault with the camera or the processing of the film. (Photograph donated by Agnes Douglas)

Right: Pat Gordon aged four, with her pram in 1919, just after the end of the First World War. She doesn't look too happy, despite being the owner of a toy pram that would make her the envy of many a wee lassie in 1919. (Photograph donated by Pat Gordon)

THREE

ENTERTAINMENT

A band playing at Waverley Market, Edinburgh, in the late 1960s. The 1950s was supposedly the decade when teenagers were invented. By the 1960s they were a force to be reckoned with; they had a very clearly-defined culture of their own. Fashion and music played an essential part, but the biggest leap forward was the fact that they had disposable income: there was money to be made – and to be spent! (Photograph donated by Gracemount Community Centre)

You can never have too much tartan. This photograph shows three of the Bay City Rollers group and three female fans. From left to right are Stuart 'Woody' Wood, Alan Longmuir, and Eric Faulkner. (Les McKeown and Derek Longmuir are missing from the picture.) The photograph was taken in 1974 when the band was beginning to make waves in the music world. There are claims that the group sold between 100 million and 300 million records. They all came from Edinburgh and the surrounding area and established their trademark with tartan scarves and clothing. By 1979 their popularity had waned dramatically and it was 'Bye-bye baby, baby bye-bye'. (Photograph donated by Seonaidh Guthrie)

Andrew Neil with his bagpipes, *c.* 1930. Andrew worked in the gunpowder factory in Roslin, about four miles outside Edinburgh. He is wearing a flat cap, a three-piece suit and is sporting a fob chain. His bagpipes hang nonchalantly under his arm, in contrast to the determined look on his face. (Photograph donated by Neil Scott)

A night out at Gorgie Dance Hall in the late 1940s. It was not common for women to go unaccompanied to the pub in that era, and it was certainly unusual for the 'pint' to be the woman's. It was the policy in some public houses to serve beer only in half pint glasses to women. (Photograph donated by Maisie Brand)

This photograph of Robert Guthrie playing his guitar in the garden at 52 Pilton Drive, Edinburgh, is signed – in pop star fashion – by the man himself. Hairstyle and glasses are very reminiscent of the Buddy Holly look. There's a traditional wooden deckchair in the background, none of your plastic garden furniture in those days. (Photograph donated by Barbara Guthrie)

A get-together at 10 Bellevue Street, Edinburgh, in 1962; some members of The Embers are present. The Embers was a local Edinburgh band, very popular in the 1960s. The original of this interior photograph is a colour Polaroid and shows bright striped curtains, pastel wallpaper decorated with shapes and a different wallpaper on the door panel; décor that was very much in vogue at the time. Colour photography was less usual then as it was still expensive for family snapshots. (Photograph donated by Jean Bell)

Brian Jones from The Rolling Stones with Alan Lunn from Edinburgh. Alan was an avid follower of Edinburgh bands in the 1960s and photographed many of them. Edinburgh also had its fair share of more famous bands playing in the city throughout this time. (Photograph donated by Willie Syme)

This photograph was taken by Alan Lunn in homage to The Beatles and shows, from the top, Jimmy Cruikshank, Peter Bottomley, Jimmy Hush, Alan Bamford, and Willie Syme. It was taken on the corner of South Clerk Street and Hope Park Terrace in Edinburgh, by Alan Lunn. The shop behind them is C. & J. Brown's, which was a well-known furniture shop in Newington; it's now a Blockbuster store. (Photograph donated by Willie Syme)

Queuing up for the matinée show at the King's Theatre at Tollcross, Edinburgh, in the late 1950s. The men in uniform are from the American Air Force base at Kirknewton. The character bending forward in the centre of the photograph is a newspaper vendor. He would sell papers at the theatre and cinema queues and also entertain with a song and dance routine. Presumably he'd stop when he ran out of papers to sell. The children are all very smartly dressed for the special occasion of their outing to the theatre. Many children in Edinburgh had their first theatre experience when they were taken to see Jimmy Logan in a pantomime at the King's Theatre. (Photograph donated by Seonaidh Guthrie)

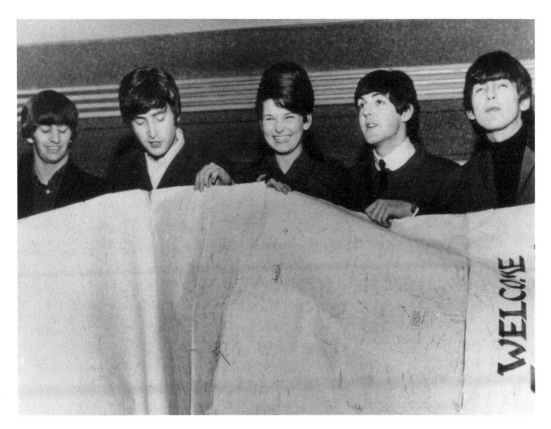

A photograph of The Beatles, visiting Edinburgh as part of their tour of Scotland in 1963. They played a concert at the ABC cinema on the corner of Lothian Road. The lucky girl with the beehive hairdo in the centre of the photograph got to present The Beatles with a giant 'Welcome to Edinburgh' card. (Photograph donated by Seonaidh Guthrie)

Open air entertainment at the Ross Bandstand in Princes Street Gardens, Edinburgh, in the late 1950s. Concerts, children's shows and Scottish country dancing were held in the Ross Bandstand, with Edinburgh Castle providing a magnificent backdrop. (Photograph donated by Seonaidh Guthrie)

Inside the Palais de Danse at Fountainbridge in the late 1950s. This photograph of the band at the Palais shows the revolving stage, fondly remembered by all those who attended. As one band finished their set, another was ready and waiting to come on. Dancing was a very popular pastime and the Palais was considered one of the best dance halls in Edinburgh; many people met their partners there. A favourite ploy of the men was to check where a lassie lived before asking if they could see her home. If it was too far away they went looking for another one! Only soft drinks were sold at the Palais, as at most dance halls. (Photograph donated by Seonaidh Guthrie)

This is a trendy Portobello hotel bar in the 1960s. Hotel bars were particularly popular when licensing laws didn't allow drinking in a public house on a Sunday. Only a 'bona fide' traveller could have a drink in a hotel bar, where they could sign the register – usually not with their own names. The drink-driving rules were less rigid in those times. The Spanish influence of the bar's appearance was no doubt inspired by the newly-popular Spanish package holidays. (Photograph donated by Joan Dougan)

FOUR

FASHION

The Haymarket bar, Edinburgh, 1960. On the left is Dorothy Craig, next to her Moira Hutchison. Both were seventeen. It's Friday night and the girls are enjoying a drink before going on to the Palais de Danse, Fountainbridge. The 1960s saw more independence for a lot of women, and for some this meant greater social freedom. A group of young women in a pub before this time would certainly have been frowned upon. Moira has obviously spent a lot of time 'back-combing'.

'This is my mother and father; they were out in my father's car, the first car he bought, and they were going up Leith Street. My mother had a new fur coat that he'd just bought for her, and my father said, "Let's go and get our picture taken, you'll not have a new fur coat often." So they went into Jerome's in Leith Street, which was not long opened then and they had their picture taken. My mother in her sealskin fur coat, big fox collar and a lovely hat with brown and white fur trim on it.' (Photograph and memory donated by Charlotte at Silverlea Day Care)

MODERN METHODS
of TAILORING SUITS
TO MEASURES

ENABLE JACKSON TO TURN OUT QUITE STYLISH GARMENTS SO LOW IN PRICE AS

84/-

Materials that are serviceable, work that is executed with great care, combined with fitting of the figure, ensure satisfaction.

JACKSON of LEITH ST.
EDINBURGH

The archaic wording of this advert is reminiscent of the public information films of the 1930s. Jackson the Tailors were in business until around the 1970s. Their styles moved with the times. Leith Street had a number of tailors' shops where you went and picked your cloth and style, and they measured you up and made your suit to measure.

Andrew Harcus and his friend, both from Faray in the Orkney Islands, pose formally in an Edinburgh studio in the 1920s. They are wearing very fine trilby hats. 'If you want to get ahead get a hat' was a slogan used by the British Hat Council in the 1930s. Hats were almost a necessity in the years until the 1960s. If you look at a photograph from a football match in the inter-war period, you'll see a sea of flat caps or 'bunnets'. (Photograph donated by Roberta Cowe)

The casual fashion shown here is the epitome of 1950s cool. This is Ted Bottomley, and his fiancée Margaret, in the front garden in Bellevue Street, Edinburgh; sunglasses were very much the fashion of the time. (Photograph donated by Jean Bell)

Ruth Dunbar photographed in the garden of 39 Northfield Crescent, Edinburgh, in 1959. The fashion was the 'new look', with the wide 'A' line skirt. Ruth also sports a short haircut, fashionable for younger women in the late 1950s and early '60s. (Photograph donated by Ronnie Dunbar)

This photograph was taken when Sandy Flockhart was working in London in 1936. This image has an almost film-star quality about it: she looks luminous. It's another good example of how well-dressed people generally were at that time. (Photograph donated by Sandy Flockhart)

'This picture was taken to record my "bargain buy" at a school jumble sale. The hat cost me sixpence and matched the colours on my jumper. The person who took the photograph became my fiancé.' (Photograph and memory donated by Betty Mackintosh)

Jerome's photographic studio in 1957; William and Jack Steel looking smart in the fashion of the day. Jerome's Studios was an Edinburgh institution and a great gauge of changing fashions from the 1930s into the late 1960s, when it eventually closed down. Located in Leith Street, it provided affordable studio portraits, at one time three photographs for 6d. The studio changed little over the years, and props and backdrops are usually recognisable as being from Jerome's. (Photograph donated by Agnes Douglas)

'This photograph was taken during typical "exam weather" when it was too nice to stay indoors and study. We used to sit on the grass reading and deluding ourselves that we were working as hard as we would have been in the University library. It was the time of poetry, Flower Power and Beautiful People, and I couldn't resist trying to get in on the act. I loved my denim trouser suit and felt really trendy in it.' (Photograph and memory donated by Norma-Ann Coleman)

A good example of how times change, not just the fashions, is how Maule's Department Store became Binns and is now House of Fraser. This Shantung coat is priced at 5 guineas, (£5 5s) and in today's money would be the equivalent of £250.

This is John O'Donnell, Donnie Lennie and their friend Tony, outside Donnie's home in Craigmillar, Edinburgh, in 1958. The lads are dressed for a night on the town; first the pub, then on to the dancing at the Palais de Danse. Long jackets were very much part of the 'Teddy Boy' style of the time. (Photograph donated by Mrs A.M. O'Donnell)

Patrick Thomson's was an Edinburgh institution; as it says in the advert: 'The store that made the Bridges famous.' It always aimed at being an up-market store, and its well-known tea room had a palm court trio to entertain the diners. Even in the 1970s, Patrick Thomson's – or PT's as it was known – still had a pneumatic tube system in place. This whisked the cash payment away from the counters and up to the counting house. Change and the receipt were placed in the cylinder and sent back to the counter for handing over to the customer.

The 1950s was a new era of prosperity for many people. Prime Minister Harold MacMillan was famous for saying: 'You've never had it so good.' People began to acquire more consumer goods such as cars and television sets, and this couple look to be the height of sophistication at a dinner dance. (Photograph donated by John McCaughie)

FIVE

WORK

Margaret McGregor standing next to a horse and cart – possibly in her home town of Wick, but it could be any of the east-coast towns associated with the herring fishing industry. Margaret was a fishwife, and was part of an 'army' of curers, fish merchants, general hands and herring lasses – or 'Gutting Quines' – who migrated from Stornoway to Great Yarmouth in pursuit of the herring. She had eleven children, nine of whom settled in Edinburgh after coming here to search for work in the 1920s. (Photograph donated by Heather Robertson)

Some of the staff from the book-binding department of McLagan & Cummings (printers), at Warriston, Edinburgh in 1920. Most of the women are wearing distinctive cuffs on their forearms as part of their uniform, because it was messy work. The printing industry employed thousands, not only in printing itself but in all the associated trades, such as paper making and book binding. As a city, Edinburgh was famous for the three Bs: Books, Barristers and Breweries. (Photograph donated by Neil Scott)

A photograph of some workers from Waterston's Sealing Wax Works in The Pleasance, Edinburgh (c. 1930). In the front row on the left is Henry Henderson, who was foreman and a sealing-wax maker, and also a quill-pen maker – one of the last quill makers in Scotland. (Photograph donated by Jim Dignall)

Above: A baker's shop in Leith, *c.* 1913. Here you can see the loaves stacked on the shelves, including half loaves. The women all have their hair in a 'bun' or 'rolls', typical of the Edwardian period and very appropriate for a bakery! You can see some weighing scales to the right, and behind the woman on the left there are glass jars containing rolls. The peculiar wrist bands are probably to protect arms from the hot ovens. Leith would at this time have been a separate municipal burgh: it merged with Edinburgh in 1920. (Photograph donated by Rena Barclay)

Right: This is a picture of Jean Combe, who worked at the Leith Ropery; she was the first female splicer here. A splicer's job was to join lengths of rope together by interweaving strands. She is wearing a new nylon uniform. Nylon was still a relatively new material when this photograph was taken in the late 1940s. Notice the typical housing of the Lochend area of Edinburgh in the background; there could even be a No. 34 bus passing by! (Photograph donated by Jean Combe)

Betty Anderson and Annie Dudgeon in their civilian pinnies, at Redford Barracks, Edinburgh, in 1946; an unknown woman stands in the middle in her ATS uniform. Betty worked in the kitchen at the barracks on Colinton Road. (Photograph donated by Betty Anderson)

Tattie howkers in the early 1950s. Picking potatoes was hard, backbreaking work and headscarves seemed compulsory. These tattie howkers are working on fields belonging to Swanston Farm – which is now a Morrisons supermarket at Hunter's Tryst. (Photograph donated by Maureen Connelly)

A man 'inking' a printing block in the 1950s. He is working at an acid etching bath, creating a printing plate for pictures. Acid etched out unwanted metal on the image to take out the 'white bits'. It is an indication of how labour-intensive the industry was – quite a contrast to high tech, modern digital printing. (Photograph donated by Joan Dougan)

A much faded and deteriorated photograph from the 1890s, showing fishing boats at the shore, Leith. In the background is the distinctive shape of the old Seaman's Mission, now the Malmasion Hotel. Leith, with its docks, was an incredibly vibrant place at this time. A wide variety of nationalities used, and passed through, Leith, making it a cosmopolitan and, at times, 'lively' area to be in. (Photograph donated by Lawrence Walker)

William Farquhar, chimney sweep, standing outside his shop at 102 The Pleasance, Edinburgh, in 1914. Alma Laing, his granddaughter, tells the rather poignant story: 'My grandfather was "called up" to join the army in 1914, but he fell off a roof while sweeping a chimney and broke his neck and died.' Notice the odd term in the window, 'practical chimney sweep', as if there was also a 'theoretical' kind! (Photograph and memory donated by Alma Laing)

'I've been in the Salvation Army all my life. My mother was a Salvationist when she was young. We were all brought up to go into the Army. There's no drink allowed in the Army, strictly teetotallers. You signed your name when you joined and you got your Articles of War with the Army flags on it. If you wanted to take it as your religion you signed it. I was collecting once for the Salvation Army in my uniform outside Jerome's the photographers in Leith Street. The women said, "Come in and we'll take your photograph for you." And here it is. They didn't charge me.' (Photograph and memory donated by Bella Reid)

A studio photograph from 1900. This is a Fisherrow fishwife from Musselburgh, carrying a creel. She is dressed in her best clothes for the photograph. When the fishwives went out selling the fish, they usually wore navy skirts and tops. This is Elizabeth Watson and the fish that she was selling would have come from her husband's boat. (Photograph donated by Elizabeth Brockie)

James Sullivan, second row down, fourth from left. James worked for a whisky bond in Leith around 1920. Edinburgh and Leith were never central to the distilling of whisky, but there were certainly plenty employed in the whisky bond warehouses and in the bottling and labelling of whisky. There are many tales of how folk managed to smuggle whisky out of the workplace, e.g. sewn in hidden pockets and the ingenious use of rubber hot water bottles! Rubber-flavoured malt whisky anyone? (Photograph donated by Jenny Middleton)

Opposite below: Part of a collection of photographs that were produced on glass quarter plates in the 1890s and 1900s. This photograph is of a prized 'Belted Galloway' bullock from a farm on the outskirts of the city. The modern parlance is 'low carbon footprint'; in plain English: food that hasn't travelled very far. At this time the majority of food was locally sourced, and the city was surrounded by market gardens and dairy and cattle farms that supplied the city directly. (Photograph donated by Lawrence Walker)

Right: Miners' cottages, The Jewel, Edinburgh, in 1959. Joan Douglas in the arms of a neighbour – resplendent in her pinny! The Jewel was one of the many outlying areas of Edinburgh that was associated with various industries. Niddrie had a brick works, Craigmillar had breweries, and Newcraighall and The Jewel had coal mining. Communities were close-knit and reliant on the workplace. Within twenty years of this photograph being taken, much had changed – mines were closed, and the industries were gone. A lot of places have been redeveloped, and retail parks, outlets, and small industrial units, have sprung up. The car is also a dominant force, with many new, busy road systems now in place. Notice the lack of cars in the street in the background of this photo. (Photograph donated by Agnes Douglas)

SIX

HOLIDAYS

Diane Kent aged eight, on holiday, in a paddling pool in 1968. Portobello, Burntisland and North Berwick were famous for their outdoor swimming pools. Portobello had a wave machine in theirs, generated by the power station which was located next to it. They were all great fun albeit freezing cold! (Photograph donated by Diane Kent)

Above: A photograph of Portobello beach, taken at the end of the 1960s. The heyday of the Great British seaside holiday was almost over. For many people, the 1970s marked the beginning of the end of holidaying in this country, as flying abroad on package deals became more common. Portobello beach was being swapped for Spanish resorts, like Costa del Sol or Benidorm, and a holiday present became a Spanish sombrero rather than a stick of seaside rock. (Photograph donated by Joan Dougan)

Left: Maureen O'Donnell, *née* Lennie, on honeymoon in Blackpool in 1957. The couple had saved up for their fare down south and stayed with Maureen's aunt. Many people couldn't afford to go on a honeymoon after getting married. Blackpool Tower looms in the background and it looks like it was a windy day on the seafront. Blackpool was a popular holiday destination for a whole generation of people from Scotland. (Photograph donated by Maureen O'Donnell)

Ella Shiels and Nan Skiven photographed on holiday in the late 1940s. There is a post-war, carefree spontaneity to this picture. Out on their bikes, roads empty of traffic, it's the perfect nostalgic snapshot. (Photograph donated by Diane Kent)

Alma Stephen on a donkey at Portobello beach, 1935. The beach was especially popular during the Glasgow Fair in July, when thousands would come from Glasgow for their annual holiday. It was also a great day trip for the locals as, in addition to the seaside, with its donkey rides and opportunities for paddling, there was a fairground to keep the family entertained. At one time it even had its own pier, sadly demolished in 1917. (Photograph donated by Alma Stephen)

Left: Robert Allan and his son Alastair on the dodgems, around 1960. Sparks used to fly from the conductor on the dodgem car as it brushed along the ceiling. The funfair was a wonderful place, with its bright lights, thrilling rides, and novelty stalls offering the chance to win a goldfish or a coconut. The goldfish, sadly, didn't usually survive long and would sometimes end up being flushed down the toilet. In the background of the picture you can see a man holding a stick with candy floss. (Photograph donated by Martha Allan)

Below: Dorothy and Valerie Craig, on holiday at Dunbar, down the coast in East Lothian, in 1957. This was an era when people didn't travel far for their summer holidays. Many Edinburgh folk went across the Forth, on the Willie Muir ferry, to Burntisland, or travelled along the east coast to Port Seton, Dunbar and North Berwick. Dorothy and Valerie were visiting the open air swimming pool in Dunbar. In the background, a man is passing with his swimming gear tucked under his arm. Dorothy is busy knitting; hopefully it isn't a pair of swimming trunks – the type inflicted on many a young boy at the time! (Photograph donated by Sharon Marshall)

A life-size photograph cut-out board, where you could pose for a humorous photograph opportunity. This one shows what happens when the man stays out to Rock Around the Clock. Blackpool was a hugely popular destination for holiday-makers in the 1950s and '60s, especially during the Glasgow Fair and the Edinburgh Trades holidays. This photograph was taken on a trip to see the Blackpool Illuminations in 1956. (Photograph donated by Seonaidh Guthrie)

Miles Tubb, on a day trip to the seaside, in 1965. He is enjoying walking barefoot on the beach, his head bent down, looking for shells to collect. It must have been a good Scottish summer as he is wearing a thick, home-knitted jumper! (Photograph donated by Miles Tubb)

Dr W. Glegg, his sister Janet Mackie, and Graham Moonie in his school uniform. They are having a picnic at Pease Bay, East Lothian, in 1931. There are three horses looking on in the background. The working harnesses indicate that they were farm horses. (Photograph donated by Graham Moonie)

Princes Street Gardens, looking towards the Mound, in 1956. It hasn't changed much over the years. People still have picnics and sunbathe in the gardens. It is a wonderful green space in the shadow of Edinburgh Castle, right in the heart of the city. (Photograph donated by Seonaidh Guthrie)

By the late 1950s and early '60s, schoolchildren were being encouraged to go on more exotic holidays. This group of teenagers were from Broughton High School and were on an organised skiing trip to Austria. There were no smart ski suits in those days. The journey to the ski resort involved four trains, the ferry from Dover to Calais, and finally a bus up a single track road with cliffs on one side and a sheer drop on the other. 'Nobody knew what an anorak or salopettes were. Mothers bought woollen trousers and knitted sweaters and provided warm jackets. The boots were hired at the ski slope. They had no previous skiing experience, so they all fell over for two weeks.' (Photograph and memory donated by Catriona Anderson)

Opposite: Alma Laing remembers: 'It was a real treat to get taken to the beach on a sunny Sunday. Everyone had the same idea and it took us forever to get to 'Porty' from our house in Prestonfield. We had to travel to the G.P.O., first by bus, and then get the tram car. The queues were miles long.' The photograph shows the children with buckets and spades, ready to make sandcastles. (Photograph and memory donated by Alma Laing)

Scout and Guide camps were popular throughout the twentieth century. Children got a chance to have a holiday, and mothers got a well-earned rest with at least some of the children away from home for a week or so during the summer months. This is a picture of the Abbey Church Girl Guides at their summer camp in 1949. The camp was held at Newstead, near North Berwick in East Lothian. (Photograph donated by Betty Reid)

Not everyone could afford to take a holiday away from home, but the long school summer holidays could still be filled with fun. Children ganged together and made the best use of communal gardens, like this one built into an Edinburgh tenement scheme. This picture was probably taken in the 1940s. Many of the children are wearing swimming costumes, perfect for being splashed with a garden hosepipe. (Photograph donated by Betty Sanderson)

This photo, taken in the mid-1950s, shows assorted family groups enjoying a summer holiday at one of the popular holiday camps, where accommodation was in chalets. Butlin's and Pontin's led the way in this holiday trend, and many people have fond memories of activities such as the Best Sandcastle championship, the Knobbly Knees competition, and the Glamorous Granny contest. Fun-filled days were organised by the Redcoats, who would then take on the evening's entertainment of community singing and ballroom dancing, obligingly partnering any unaccompanied ladies round the dance floor. (Photograph donated by Edward Wright)

Portobello beach in the 1950s. Only two miles from Edinburgh, it was a popular place for a day trip. In this photograph a family from Edinburgh enjoy a picnic together. (Photograph donated by Sadie Maxwell)

SEVEN

SPORT

A rather posed photograph from 1905, taken at Bell's Mill, near Dean Village. The men are properly attired in the cycling wear of the day. This was a golden age of cycling, very much celebrated in the Alan Bennett play *A Day Out*. (Photograph donated by Lawrence Walker)

Boxing was a popular amateur and professional sport for much of the twentieth century. The two big Edinburgh clubs were Sparta and Leith Victoria. Here we see James and John Watson outside Sparta Athletic Club in Macdonald Road, around 1950. James went on to become Scottish boxing champion. The Sparta Club narrowly avoided closure recently when it was forced out of its Macdonald Road premises. It is now in Dryden Street. (Photograph donated by Maureen Watson)

This picture shows a keep-fit group from the 1920s. On the top of the pyramid is Peter Addison, and in support (left to right) are Jimmy Maconachie, Bob Williamson and Willie Morris. Willie and Bob were members of Edinburgh Harriers' Athletic Club. The 1920s and '30s saw quite a vogue for keep-fit. The Women's League of Health & Beauty started in the 1930s. On a much more sinister level, in the 1930s, was the Nazis' obsession with the body beautiful. (Photograph donated by Nan Gray)

Milton Amateur Wrestling Club, Abbeyhill, in 1962. Jim Dignall says: 'In the photograph I am on my back – my usual wrestling position – with Ronnie McKenzie showing the hold. The facilities at the club were spartan: a wrestling mat, free weights, an Ascot gas water-heater for showers and no heating! It required a lot of dedication.' Wrestling on the television in the 1960s became compulsive viewing for many people, especially women. There were many stars who attracted their own followers – Mick McManus, Jackie Pallo and Giant Haystacks. (Photograph donated by Maggi and Jim Dignall)

Fore! This golfer cuts a dashing figure on the course with his snazzy windbreaker and plus-fours. It's a photograph from the 1930s and it looks like it was posed for, rather than taken after an actual shot. (Photograph donated by Graham Moonie)

Members of Leith Victoria Athletic Club pictured with their trophies at the end of a successful season. Leith Victoria is Scotland's oldest boxing club and has recently had its building refurbished in Academy Street. It was founded in 1919 for workers from Victoria Docks. (Photograph donated by Nettie Mckay)

A swimming club (possibly from Dalry Baths) pictured on Portobello Beach in 1922. A really mixed group of swimmers in the universal one-piece costumes of the time. The man on the left stands justifiably proud, with his finely-honed physique. (Photograph donated by Andrew Vardy)

A bathing beauties' competition at Portobello indoor baths in the late 1940s. Catherine Sutherland is in the centre foreground of the photograph. At that time, Mrs Sutherland was one of only three people who held a Life Saving Badge in the UK. She taught swimming in Portobello and then in Aberdeen. In the background, a young girl covers her face with her hands, possibly embarrassed by the whole thing; perhaps her mother is one of the competitors. (Photograph donated by Mrs C. Dickie)

The Newtongrange Rockets were a local speedway team. Early records show that speedway racing may have taken place at Newtongrange in Midlothian as early as 1928. What is certain, is that racing did take place at the Victoria Park Stadium in the early 1950s and again in the 1970s. This was a popular sport in the post-war years in Edinburgh. The speedway club in Edinburgh was known as the Monarchs and was based at Meadowbank Stadium. (Photograph donated by Martha Allan)

The Edinburgh Dynamos were a very popular women's football team in the late 1940s and '50s. Their home ground was at Meadowbank Stadium. At one game against Bolton Ladies FC at Meadowbank, they played in front of a 10,000 plus crowd – the sort of crowd capacity that modern-day Hibs or Hearts would be envious of.

A fine collection of shorts and knees! The Dynamos were about to play Preston Ladies' Football Team. Unfortunately they lost 6-2. This photograph was taken in 1952. (Photograph donated by Bet Adamson)

Musselburgh Cycle Club at Coldingham Youth Hostel, Berwickshire, in 1953. Grace Melrose is in the centre of the photograph. She says: 'In the winter and early spring, cyclists often went hostelling and rode time trials during the racing season. This was our last weekend hostelling as we were emigrating to Canada on 5 April 1953. Robert, my husband of about two weeks, took the photograph. Our bikes already had new owners.' (Photograph donated by Grace Melrose)

George Farquhar, Neil Lumsden and James Dignall, in 1962, on the side of Castlelaw Hill in the Pentlands. James says: 'It was a very hard winter with deep snow; so much we were able to ski over a totally hidden five-bar gate! We skied from Hillend to Flotterstone, then back along the Carlops Road, which was blocked with snow.' (Photograph donated by James Dignall)

Right: Early 1970s at Wallyford Dog Track near Musselburgh. Greyhound racing was a popular sport in Edinburgh up until the 1980s, and the main Edinburgh dog racing track was at Powderhall. The stadium was a popular venue, not only for the dogs, but also for speedway and the annual Powderhall sprint (for men), which took place on New Year's Day. (Photograph donated by Joan Dougan)

Below: An Edwardian sports club, or perhaps a work outing; this is an intriguing photograph with an unknown history. Part of the fun of such an image is working out what might have been going on. The dress is formal, but in amongst the finery is a cricket bat and a medicine ball. If it is a work outing then the workplace or department must have employed more women than men. Parts of the printing trade were biased toward employing women. An anonymous moment of enjoyment captured forever! (Photograph donated by Joan Dougan)

The looser, more informal, fashions of the 1920s allowed a bit more freedom of movement. These young women are enjoying a 'round' on the putting green at North Berwick. Their clothing is not dissimilar to what was being worn by women tennis players at Wimbledon at the time. (Photograph donated by Heather Pont)

This photograph was taken in the 1980s, when skateboarding first became popular in the UK. This temporary ramp could possibly be in the grounds of Gracemount House as the image comes from a collection by the Gracemount Youth Club. Fashion moves on though; no respectable youth would be seen in those shorts now!

An athletic pose taken in a photographer's studio. William Millar boxed before the First World War. His hands are strapped or 'handwrapped'. This is a procedure that all boxers go through before putting on their gloves, and is done to protect their hands from the impact of punching. William not only boxed, but also worked on the railway during the day and at the theatre in the evening. (Photograph donated by Betty Anderson)

EIGHT

STREET LIFE

Edinburgh Castle. This was a publicity postcard for Green's Hairdresser in Castle Street, Edinburgh, and was taken by Jas A. Brydon, who was a professional photographer. He has contributed many fine images to the LMA archive and to this book. In the photograph you can see cars parked on Princes Street – not something you would see now. (Photograph donated by Joan Dougan)

Coronation Day in Hen's Dyke, Dumbiedykes. Hen's Dyke was an elevated concrete 'green' with steps leading down to Dumbiedykes Road. At the back of the group of neighbours you can see the awnings of the local Co-op stores. The brick building at the right-hand side is the bleach works. The street has been spruced up for the occasion with what look like Christmas decorations. There's a real sense of community spirit in this photograph as they all share the celebration for Queen Elizabeth's Coronation: many of the children are wearing what appear to be paper crowns. (Photograph donated by Jean Bell)

Woolworths in all its splendour, at the east end of Princes Street, 1957. 'Woolies' was well known for having 'things for a tanner'; this one had a popular café on the second floor. The flowers on the street, and the flags decorating the outside of the store, were there to welcome a visiting member of the royal family. The photograph was taken by a Kodak Bantam and the original was in colour. (Photograph donated by Sarah Knight)

The west end of Princes Street, looking east. St John's Church is on the right at the bottom of Lothian Road and a policeman is directing the traffic. The awnings are out over the shops to shade the windows from the sun. The date is 1956 and the reason for the road works was the removal of the tram lines. The west end looks a bit drab, with makeshift barriers in place due to the road works – not too dissimilar to the state it's in now with the re-introduction of the tram service. (Photograph donated by Seonaidh Guthrie)

Above: The view from one of the twin tower blocks, Grampian or Cairngorm, in Leith. These high-rise blocks were built in 1962 and were demolished in 1997. They offered a panoramic view over the Forth to Fife. The photograph shows Newhaven pier and, on the horizon, the old fishing port of Granton. In the foreground is the Caledonian railway line, which went as far as Canonmills. The land around Newhaven has been reclaimed for development, with new housing, shopping amenities and superstores being built. (Photograph donated by George Hackland)

Right: This was taken by a street photographer in Princes Street in 1935. Street photographers had pitches throughout the city and would take photographs of people and then ask if they wanted to buy a copy. Their pictures are perfect time pieces, which capture people going about their everyday lives – or perhaps on a special day out. Here Ada and Elsie Webster are elegantly dressed, both with hats, gloves and handbags, on a trip uptown. Elsie is wearing a fur coat, which even for the time would have been considered quite a luxury. (Photograph donated by Betty Mackintosh)

An image collected from a box of old photographs found at Gorgie Memorial Halls. Details are scant, but it was probably taken in the Gorgie-Dalry area of the city in the 1920s. It is not a school photograph but a 'back green' photograph. These images were often taken by itinerant photographers, who would gather the kids of the area together to take a group photo. The hope was to sell copies to the parents. These children look a little happier than those in the Dr Bell's school photo; this could be because they are out and about, playing. The children are of varying ages and fairly well dressed: some of the boys are wearing jackets and ties. Notice the boy on the right of the middle row, sitting astride a tricycle; the wee girl at the front wearing her tackety boots; and the other wee girl next to her with spectacles. (Photograph donated by Andrew Vardy)

Mary Dunlop was a well-known figure around the West End in the 1940s and 1950s. She is pictured here with Smokey, her pony. Smokey would pull the barrel organ around the streets and Mary would turn the handle and collect pennies from the public. (Photograph donated by Jean Bell)

A street party held on 2 June 1953, in Newton Street, Gorgie, to celebrate the Coronation of Queen Elizabeth II. People would dress up for these occasions; all of the children in this photograph are wearing party hats and their best clothes. The streets would be closed to traffic; tables, chairs and tablecloths would be brought out and people would sit down to eat, drink and celebrate together. The Coronation was the first major national event to be broadcast on television. Many people remember it as being the first time they actually watched a television set, often the only one in a street. (Photograph donated by Andrew Vardy)

This is taken from the top balcony at 42 Dumbiedykes Road, Edinburgh. The poor housing in the Dumbiedykes area was redeveloped in the 1960s. Some of the lads in the photograph went on to start up a local band called The Embers, which proved quite popular in Edinburgh. In the background, the new tower blocks for residential accommodation are being constructed. These 'new builds' were later refurbished in 2007 as the area went 'upmarket' with the coming of the tourist attraction, Dynamic Earth, the new offices for the *Scotsman* newspaper, and, of course, the Scottish Parliament building. (Photograph donated by Jean Bell)

A group of friends (*c.* 1958). These were the days of short trousers, long socks and standard haircuts; short back and sides. It was also a time when kids played outside and had to be called in for their tea, or when it got too dark. Happy days – and not a girl in sight. (Photograph donated by Ronnie Dunbar)

This photograph is taken from a room in the North British Hotel, now the Balmoral Hotel, at the east end of Princes Street, looking west. Down below is Waverley Station, and the Scott Monument is the gothic structure straight ahead. The couple are posed gazing out of the open window. This picture was taken in the early 1950s, before hotel rooms had televisions. (Photograph donated by Joan Dougan)

Left: Peter Bottomley, aged three, photographed around 1950 in the back green of 38 Dumbiedykes Road, Edinburgh. The balconies were a feature of the new, improved housing in Dumbiedykes. There's a pram in the background, which would probably have been used to carry the washing to and from the wash-house at Simon Square, before being pegged out on the line in the shared drying green. The area of Dumbiedykes is close to the development of the new Scottish Parliament building. (Photograph donated by Jean Bell)

Below: The floral clock in Princes Street Gardens is a famous Edinburgh landmark during the summertime, when it comes into bloom. It is believed to be the oldest floral clock in the world. The clock is replanted with a different design every spring, in preparation for the summer. Every year since 1946, the floral clock has celebrated a different event or anniversary. The year this picture was taken, 1958, the floral clock celebrated the centenary of the Edinburgh Royal Choral Union and some of the passing crowd appear interested – others seem somewhat blasé about it. (Photograph donated by Seonaidh Guthrie)

On the balcony of 19 Johnstone Street, Leith, with (left to right) Mary Robertson, Jean Wilson, and Mrs Cunningham. Number 19 was a red brick building owned by A. & R. Hepburn Engineers, of Dock Street, Leith. The tenement was built over Hepburn's workshops. It had a flat roof that could be used as a drying area for the washing. This picture captures beautifully a moment in domestic life, with one of the women (Jean) making her point by wagging her finger. We can only guess at what she might be saying, but it's likely to be a comment about Mary, seated in the front. (Photograph donated by Heather Pont)

An everyday postcard image of Princes Street in the 1950s, looking west over Waverley Station, showing the castle on the hill and the Royal Scottish Academy and National Gallery buildings at the bottom of the Mound. The shop on the right, with all the awnings, is R.W. Forsyth's, an up-market outfitters and clothes shop (long since closed), which supplied many a schoolchild with their uniform requirements, from caps and blazers to gym slips and sensible shoes. (Photograph donated by Evelyn Muir)

This photograph was taken from Waterloo Place, Edinburgh, around 1900. Today, the statue of the Duke of Wellington on his horse is still outside General Register House, at the east end of Princes Street, although people's fashions have changed quite a bit since the turn of the last century. Nearly everyone in the photograph is wearing a hat and the style of dress, for both men and women, was much more formal. (Photograph donated by Eva Butler)

The old makes way for the new. In the 1960s, George Square saw extensive redevelopment. A new tower block – David Hume Tower, part of Edinburgh University's new teaching facilities – looms in the background. In the George Square and Bristo Street area was Parker's stores, with its distinctive Tudor-style frontage, which many older Edinburgh residents still remember. (Photograph donated by Jenny Middleton)

Josie is on the left with ribbons in her hair. She is pictured with her Aunt Paulette who is cradling Josie's cousin, James. Josie doesn't look too happy in the photograph and neither does cousin James, who is very tightly cocooned in swaddling clothes. The photograph was taken in the back green of a tenement in East Thomas Street, at the top of Leith Walk, in the late 1940s. This area was known locally as 'China town' and was redeveloped in the 1970s. (Photograph donated by Josie Sawyer)

The Canongate in the 1950s. The building by the bus stop is Huntly House, which is now the home of the Museum of Edinburgh. Opposite is the old Canongate Tolbooth, which was built in 1591. It was here that the tolls or public dues were collected. It also served as the Council House, courtroom and prison for the burgh of Canongate (although most of the prisoners were transferred to a newly-built jail on Calton Hill). It is now the site of The People's Story Museum. In the 1950s the Canongate was a residential and working area, with many shops, breweries, and printer's works, as well as tenement flats. (Photograph donated by Craiglockhart Lunch Club)

The end of Shandwick Place, looking toward Princes Street and Lothian Road. The church is St John's. Building-wise it is not a scene that has changed a great deal, although Binns the department store, on the left, is now Frasers. The building had a famous clock, around which figures circled on the hour – the clock is just out of the shot. 'Binns corner under the clock' was a favourite place for courting couples to meet. There is the rather cruel story told of the woman who arranges to meet a blind date 'under the clock'. She stays on the bus as it goes along Shandwick Place, just to check the man out. She decides she doesn't like the look of him and doesn't get off. (Photograph donated by J. Dustan)

White Horse Close, at the bottom of the Royal Mile, in the 1950s. The 'Close' is now gentrified, but fifty years ago it would have been part of the 'Old Town' community, which would have been working class. The photograph shows a typical scene: children playing, babies in prams and mothers hanging out washing. This is a historic part of the city. The Royal Mews was situated here in the sixteenth century. It was subsequently known as Davidson's Close and Laurence Ord's Close, and received its current name when Ord built an inn and named it in honour of Queen Mary's white palfrey. (Photograph donated by Craiglockhart Lunch Club)

Part of the frontage of Parker's Stores in Bristo Street, in the late 1950s. The mock half-timbered frontage of Parker's was a bit of an oddity in Edinburgh. The store, however, was very popular, and in its various departments sold clothes, school uniforms, and haberdashery. It seems to have had an almost permanent sale advertised in its windows, and it was certainly renowned for its bargain prices. The area was extensively redeveloped in the 1960s and, along with many other popular businesses, Parker's was pulled down. The area around Bristo Square is now associated with the University of Edinburgh, as many of the buildings belong to them. (Photograph donated by J. Dustan)

Above: Brunswick Street, at the top of Leith Walk, in the 1960s. This was another area of the city where the housing had become very run-down. This photograph shows the tenements abandoned and boarded up, prior to demolition. The walls are covered in graffiti 'celebrating' one of the local gangs, the Easter Road Boot Boys, and stating that 'China town is a no go area'. The area was known as China town possibly because of visiting sailors, who were accommodated there. (Photograph donated by Calton Centre)

Above: The royal visit of George VI to Edinburgh in 1937. We are looking down the Mound to Princes Street. It's another view that would be instantly recognisable today: the large building on the right is the Royal Scottish Academy, still in use now. This was George VI's first visit to Scotland after his Coronation, and he stayed for seven days at Holyrood Palace. Royal visits were hugely popular events and thousands lined the street to view the royal procession and mounted guard. A ceremony was held in Holyrood Park, where a large crowd covered the lower slopes of Salisbury crags. Tram rails and overhead cables are just visible in the photo. (Photograph donated by Jessie Lamont)

Right: Taken from the foot of Hanover Street, looking up towards George Street. The ornate archway had been erected to celebrate the Coronation of Edward VII in 1902. The scene looks to be largely devoid of people. However, there are three photographers grouped around their tripods and cameras. They are in the process of taking a photograph, and their image would include in it the very person who took this photograph! If you look closely you will see there are more figures, faint blurs of people on the move. As with many photographs of this period, the exposure time would take a while. Any fast movement would not be recorded at all, or would become a blur – which is why a seemingly empty street is inhabited by ghosts! (Photograph donated by Lawrence Walker)

NINE

WARTIME

A photograph of the Homeguard in 1939. Our perception of the Homeguard may have been coloured by its portrayal in the 1970s' comedy series, *Dad's Army*. In reality, 'Local Defence Volunteers' – as they were originally called – were an important part of the home defence strategy. Volunteers were charged with defending their local area. This group were workers from the Bruce Peebles' factory, which manufactured transformers and generators – important for the war effort. (Photograph donated by Barbara Guthrie)

Here we see workers taking a break from duties in the gunpowder factory in Roslin during the First World War. The men are wearing protective clothing made of felt but the women, who probably worked in the packing department, only appear to have been given pinafores to cover their day dresses. The factory in Roslin was in production for 150 years and was, at one time, the largest in Scotland. (Photograph donated by Neil Scott)

Right: Maisie on a tractor in Hawick, 1942. With so many men called up to the armed forces, women were drafted in to take their place at work. The important role that women played during wartime has only recently being officially acknowledged. Food production was of vital importance for life on the home front. Many women joined the Land Army and were put to work on farms; driving tractors, planting and harvesting. The rural life could sometimes come as a shock for a 'city girl'. It was hard, exhausting work in the fields. (Photograph donated by Maisie Brand)

Below: This is one of the strangest photographs we have in the archive. Some people find it funny, others disturbing. It is a gas attack training exercise at Shrubhill bus depot in 1939. The line up includes Bunty Bishop's father, although she is unable to pick him out. The threat of a gas attack was very real after the horrors of the First World War. Children were issued with gas masks and would take them to school. (Photograph donated by Bunty Bishop)

Above: This photograph was taken outside Dalry Primary School, on 3 September 1939, at the outbreak of the Second World War. The children are carrying gas masks and are ready to be evacuated to the safety of the countryside. The Forth estuary was the target of one of the first air raids, and fears of bombings in Edinburgh were high. Fortunately, Edinburgh was not badly hit by air raids and many of the children who were evacuated returned to the city within a few weeks. People who lived through the war talk of rationing, blackouts and air-raid signals, but they also say that life went on, and there was still the cinema and dancing to get you through. (Photograph donated by Andrew Vardy)

Left: David Scott is pictured here, in a convalescence uniform, after being wounded in the First World War. The Flora Stevenson School in Comely Bank was used as a hospital for wounded soldiers. David is pictured against a backdrop in a photographer's studio. (Photograph donated by Neil Scott)

There were two types of structures synonymous with the Second World War: the air-raid shelter and the prefab. This photograph, taken in 1946, shows both of them. Prefabs, or prefabricated houses, were a quick fix for the chronic housing shortage after the war. Prefabricated sections were bolted together on-site, and a complete house was constructed within days. The prefabs are still standing, and indeed being lived in, in the Moredun area of Edinburgh. The small brick-built building next to the prefab is an Anderson Shelter. This would be used when the air-raid siren sounded, as it offered more protection against the bombs. (Photograph donated by Maureen Connelly)

John Maley, called up to the Fleet Air Arm in 1942, is pictured here kitted out in a pilot's uniform. John says: 'Although I was just an Air Mechanic (A) Airframes, I enjoyed going up with the pilots on test flights. My favourite plane was the open cockpit Swordfish, affectionately known throughout the Fleet as 'the Stringbag'. We did a five-week training course and our instructor was Leading Seaman Hopkins, a survivor from a tribal class destroyer. When we finished the training we shook his hand and told him how glad we were to be leaving. He said, "Some day you'll wish you were back here."' (Photograph donated by John Maley)

Dorothy Macintosh in the Auxiliary Territorial Service (ATS) in 1943. The ATS was the women's branch of the British Army during the Second World War. It was formed on 9 September 1938, initially as a women's voluntary service, and lasted just over ten years. Women were not eligible to serve on the front-line, but members of the ATS and other women's voluntary services were needed to help with ancillary roles, such as radar operators and as part of the team of anti-aircraft guns. (Photograph donated by Dorothy Macintosh)

Above: A wartime wedding photograph in Granton, 1942. Weddings would be organised around the time the man was due to get his leave from the forces. They were usually small affairs with the reception held at home. The mother of the bride and the sister would give their clothing rations to the bride so that she could buy a nice wedding dress or going-away outfit. (Photograph donated Alma Stephen)

Left: Thomas Macintosh in full Biggles' gear photographed in 1942. Thomas was an RAF reconnaissance photographer and he was clearly very proud of his state of the art camera. (Photograph donated by Dorothy Macintosh)

This is Marcelle, Marian and Arthur Payne, in their back garden, wearing gas masks during the Second World War. It looks as if the children are wearing adult gas masks. Children did have their own gas masks, however, which they had to take to school every day. There were also special cradle-like respirators for babies. (Photograph donated by Marian Thom)

The boys are home on leave; their sweethearts and their friends in reserved occupations are determined to show them a good time. Notice how some of the couples have exchanged hats, with two of the girls showing off the soldiers' berets and the soldiers gamely wearing their girlfriends' bonnets. This pleasant outing took place in Roslin sometime between 1914 and 1918. (Photograph donated by Neil Scott)

A photograph from 1870. John Maley says: 'On the left is my grandfather, John Hay; next to him is my great-grandfather, who is seated, and the other person is his friend. My great-grandfather joined the British army as a bandsman in 1854 at Dunbar Barracks.' John Maley was also in the services. He joined the Fleet Air Arm in the Second World War. (Photograph donated by John Maley)

Maisie Brand marching in a Land Army parade in 1943. The government was required to increase food production as the prospect of the war became more likely. The Women's Land Army was started in June 1939 in order to provide the help that would be needed to grow more food on Britain's farms. The Land Girls came from the countryside and the cities; Edinburgh girls travelled to farms in East Lothian and the borders. Life in the country would prove to be an eye-opener for lots of the city girls. (Photograph donated by Maisie Brand)

Above: Grace Melrose's father-in-law, Alex Melrose, proudly displays his uniform of the Local Defence Volunteers in October 1939. The medals and ribbons on Alex's uniform were from the First World War, including the Military Medal awarded to him for his service in the Dardanelles. Also in the picture are young Robert Melrose, Marjorie Melrose – who joined the WAAFs in 1943 – and Stanley Melrose, who went on to join the Royal Engineers and worked in Bomb Disposal. (Photograph donated by Grace Melrose)

Left: This unusual photograph shows a group of soldiers kitted out for service in Norway during the First World War. The soldiers were lodged in Edinburgh prior to being mobilised. Tom Young, seated on the left, stayed with Mrs M. Watson's parents in Saughton Mains. (Photograph donated by Mrs M. Watson)

Betty Anderson was part of the first mixed gun battery set up during the Second World War. Her initial training took place in Scotland and then she was posted to various camps in England and Wales. In this picture, Betty can be seen second from the right with other colleagues outside their barrack huts. (Photograph donated by Betty Anderson)

This picture was taken in Korea in 1953. The King's Own Scottish Borderers are preparing for manoeuvres in the war in Korea. William Pringle – Susan Pringle's husband – is on the left of the picture, and on the right is George Mackenzie, who played for Hibernian Football Club. The Korean War is sometimes referred to as the 'Forgotten War'. (Photograph donated by Susan Pringle)

TEN

TRANSPORT

Buses on parade. A delivery of new buses, in their distinctive madder (dark red) and white livery, at Edinburgh Corporation Transport depot – now Lothian Regional Transport depot – in Annandale Street in 1960. This site would have been a bus-spotter's paradise. The buses have sequential number plates, so they don't get lost! Lothian Buses Plc is the only municipal bus company in Scotland. The company can trace its history back to the Edinburgh Street Tramways Company of 1871. The city's bus transport will integrate with the new trams – when they arrive. (Photograph donated by Joan Dougan)

A photograph from the 1950s, showing the interior of the supports of the Forth Railway Bridge, between South and North Queensferry. We presume they were carrying out maintenance checks on the structure of the bridge. Work on building the Forth Railway Bridge began in 1882 and it was opened in 1890. It's a cantilever bridge built out of steel, with three distinctive diamond-shaped towers. This new cantilever design for the bridge was required after the 1879 Tay Bridge disaster, when the bridge collapsed, killing seventy-five people. The photograph is quite surreal and wouldn't look out of place in a Hitchcock movie, or as part of a dream sequence from the German Expressionist period. (Photograph donated by Joan Dougan)

A St Cuthbert's Co-op horse-drawn milk cart, photographed in Lauderdale Street. Milk continued to be delivered by horse and cart to some areas of Edinburgh into the mid-1970s. The horse would follow the same delivery route, day in and day out; and there were regular customers who would feed it tit-bits as it passed by. Notice that milk churns were also still being used, although most of the milk appears to be being delivered in re-usable glass bottles. (Photograph donated by Miss A.B. Laidlaw)

The Edinburgh Corporation Transport bus depot and workshop at Shrubhill, off Leith Walk, in the 1960s. Most Edinburgh buses were double-decker, manned by a driver and conductor, but this photograph shows one of the rarer single-decker buses, undergoing repair work. The Shrubhill workshop was located between Edinburgh and Leith and housed the haulage engines for the old tram system. (Photograph donated by Joan Dougan)

'My Grandfather, William Williamson, is the conductor on the left in the photo. He came from Fair Isle and worked on the horse-drawn trams when he first arrived in Edinburgh.' The tram is advertising the Empire Theatre in Nicolson Street, a popular nightspot for an evening's entertainment. The photograph was taken around 1900. The tram ran from Pilrig to Gorgie, via Princes Street and St Andrews Street. (Photograph and memory donated by Nan Gray)

Norma-Ann Coleman remembers: 'An early memory of Cowan Road (Edinburgh) was the store horse standing patiently in the street in all weathers, while the milkman clambered up the tenement stairs delivering pints of milk. You never forget the thrill of buying your first house. Mine was a one-bedroomed flat in a tenement in Cowan Road and cost £7,800 when I bought it in 1975.' This photograph shows the horse waiting in the snow, early in the morning before the gritters had been out. (Photograph and memory donated by Norma-Ann Coleman)

This photograph was taken at the Craigentinny railway sidings, in the late 1950s. Georgina Reynolds is in the centre of the back row. Helen (Georgina's daughter) writes: 'The empty trains from Waverley Station went down to Craigentinny sidings to be cleaned; both the ordinary and the sleeper carriages. The women worked shifts 6 a.m. to 2 p.m., 2 p.m. to 10 p.m. and nightshift.' The women are wearing overalls and dungarees as the work was dirty. (Photograph and memory donated by Helen Reynolds)

Billy Fiddler emerges from the shadows of an Iberia Airways plane in 1965. This is transport of a whole different kind! At this time, foreign package holidays were beginning to take off – literally – and Edinburgh Airport, formerly RAF Turnhouse, began to market itself as a commercial airport. In 2009 Edinburgh Airport was used by over 9 million passengers. (Photograph donated by Billy Fiddler)

George Hackland writes: 'This is my father, J.C. Hackland, sitting in my Uncle George's car. My uncle George Craig had a boot and shoe shop on the corner of Chambers Street and he supplied surgical boots to the Royal Infirmary.' The car is an unusual one, a Bean Car, built to rival the Model T Ford; this looks like a Bean four-seater touring model. They were produced in Dudley, Worcestershire between 1919 and 1929. (Photograph and memory donated by George Hackland)

Len Purves takes the reins; Fife coast, 1959. The pony and trap (donkey in this case), was a common mode of transport right up to the Second World War – particularly in rural areas. By the 1950s, however, it had been relegated to a seaside attraction. Such was its novelty – and the placid nature of the donkey – that it holds the children's rapt attention. (Photograph donated by Len Purves)

The bridge that goes nowhere! It's 1963 and the Forth Road Bridge was under construction; building had started in 1958. Prior to this, the crossings from South to North Queensferry were made by ferry – latterly SS *The Queen Margaret*. Such is the volume of traffic in recent years that there is a strong likelihood of a second road-bridge being built. (Photograph donated by Jenny Middleton)

The opening of the Forth Road Bridge on 4 September 1964. The bridge had caused great excitement and crowds gathered to cross on the opening day; the official opening ceremony was carried out by the Queen. Oddly, we have never seen any images of the first car crossing the bridge! (Photograph donated by Jenny Middleton)

Ian D. Macleod astride a BSA motorbike in 1969. Motorcycling was certainly a cheaper form of transport than driving. Models ranged from the humble scooter or moped, to this fine 'ton up' model, which represents the best and most expensive of British bikes at the time. The British bike industry was the world leader until the 1960s, with Triumph and Norton – as well as BSA – being the most popular. However, because of a lack of investment and foresight, it was superseded by the Japanese industry in the 1970s. There was even an Edinburgh motorcycle manufacturer in the Powderhall area of Edinburgh in the early part of twentieth century. (Photograph donated by Nan Macleod)

An upturned coal lorry at an unknown location in the 1920s. In hilly cities like Edinburgh, it was common for there to be reports of 'runaway' lorries or lorry loads tipping. As we can see from this image on a steep incline, the load has shifted to the back of the truck and tipped the whole vehicle. Arthur Street, in the Southside of Edinburgh, was particularly notorious for this type of problem and there are quite a few tales of buckets of spilt coal being whisked away for the home fire. (Photograph donated by Miles Tubb)

The last tram to run from Portobello to the GPO building at the east end of Princes Street, Edinburgh. Councillor Stanley is in the back of the photo, in the centre, wearing the smart overcoat. Next to him, on the right, is Charlie Turner, a Portobello hairdresser. The two women in the centre at the front are Rhona Lindsay (left) and Anne Ramage. Edinburgh's tram system was abandoned in November 1956 and the whole complex rail and cabling system was removed. Trams were seen as old-fashioned! (Photograph donated by Rhona Brown)

A Post Office delivery van and driver, *c.* 1934. The Post Office or General Post Office (GPO) was central to communication in Britain at this time. As well as the postal delivery – the Royal Mail – the Post Office ran the telegram and telephone services. Motorised transportation was an important part of their work, using not only vans but motorcycles as well. However, the bulk of the mail being transported long distances was carried by train. This was famously documented in the 1936 film *Night Mail*, about a London, Midland & Scottish Railway (LMS) mail train from London to Scotland; the poem by W.H. Auden was specially written to accompany the film.

Opposite above: Vespa and Lambretta motor scooters gained a certain notoriety during the 1960s, with their popularity amongst 'Mods'. However, in the 1950s, the motor scooter was just another form of cheap transport. Because of its riding position, you could sit with your knees together rather than sitting astride; it proved popular with women riders, as seen in this photo. (Photograph donated by Craigentinny Lunch Club)

Opposite below: This was taken in a photographer's studio around 1890; it is quite an oddity. The picture shows a wonderfully-detailed painted back drop of Princes Street, looking eastward from the Mound, and shows the scene of a typical pony and trap of the time; it could have almost been taken outside. What the scene was meant to portray, with the barefooted boy holding the reins, is a mystery, as it is likely that the children in the photograph were from a relatively wealthy background. There is also what appears to be a number plate attached to the trap. (Photograph donated anonymously)

Other titles published by The History Press

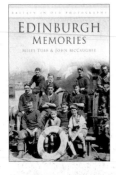

Edinburgh Memories
MILES TUBB & JOHN MCCAUGHIE

Edinburgh Memories is the unique and fascinating result of many conversations and interviews with local people, recalling life in the city between the wars. Compiled by the Living Memory Association, it contains vivid memories and tales of childhood and schooldays, work and play, sport and leisure, and the war years. Anyone who knows Edinburgh, as a resident or a visitor, will be amused and entertained, surprised and moved by these stories, which capture the unique spirit of Scotland's capital city.

978 0 7509 5100 5

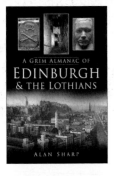

A Grim Almanac of Edinburgh and the Lothians
ALAN SHARP

Beneath the surface respectability lies a warren of filth-ridden alleys where thieves, murderers and ghouls of every description planned and carried out their foul deeds. In this book we meet them all. Major Weir, the devil-worshipping black magician and his wicked sister Grizel; Captain Porteous, the corrupt official who inspired the population to mob justice; and, of course, Mr Burke and Mr Hare, who plied their swift trade in corpses for the dissection table of Dr Knox.

978 0 7509 5105 0

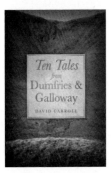

Ten Tales from Dumfries & Galloway
DAVID CARROLL

Dumfries and Galloway can boast Scotland's highest village, Wanlockhead; while Kirkcudbright and its surrounding area witnessed the growth of a thriving artists' community in the late nineteenth and early twentieth century. Tragedy on a large scale has struck the region more than once, while the discovery of a sulphurous well in a small Annandale village transformed Moffat into the 'Cheltenham of Scotland'. Illustrated with over fifty pictures, these and other fascinating stories can all be found in *Ten Tales from Dumfries & Galloway*.

978 0 7509 4419 9

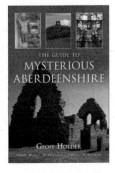

The Guide to Mysterious Aberdeenshire
GEOFF HOLDER

This fascinating guide offers an invaluable insight into the mysterious Scottish county of Aberdeenshire. Every historic site and ancient monument is explored, along with the many hidden treasures to be found in the area. With everything from beautiful ruins, stone circles and eerie sculptures to the wickerman covered, this is an indispensable companion for anyone about to journey into the mysterious realms of Aberdeenshire.

978 0 7524 4988 3

Visit our website and discover thousands of other History Press books.
www.thehistorypress.co.uk